In Search of

Poetry Collection

Danuta Dagair

LONDON 2017

ISBN-13: 978-1544617848
ISBN-10:1544617844

DEDICATION

I dedicate this book to my loved ones, thanks to whom it was created. It is you, my dears, who were my inspiration for writing poetry, and you, who by giving me the continuous possibility of enjoying your presence with me, are helping me further with discovering the joy and meaning in my life.

To Jim

from Danuta Dagair

DDag

dn. 18.09.2022

PREFACE

This book contains a total of 64 poems, which depending on their subject matter, are divided into four parts: I - Beauty of nature, II - Fun and positive emotions, III - In a family circle, IV - Romantic sphere: dreams and feelings.

Their topics are varied, depending on the situation, mood, or thoughts associated with writing them, and which at the time gave me the impetus to create a specific poem. You can find therein sadness and joy, melancholy and hope for the better future, as well as critical threads or indulgence, connected with understanding of human flaws and frailties.

And, also, you will find in them the reflection of a variety of life experiences collected throughout my life so far. I believe, the reader, you will recognize imprints of such moments from your own life; those cheerful and sorrowful, solemn and frivolous, melancholic and jocular, worthy of admiration or reflection, maybe even a change. I hope I will not fail you.

ACKNOWLEDGMENTS

I would like to thank those who helped me to correct mistakes that as a foreigner I could not notice on my own.

The biggest thanks are to Cindy Glover, who was very encouraging at the beginning of my writing, giving me a helping hand, when I needed it the most.

I am also much thankful to my daughter, Luiza, who helped me to manage the technical issues of publishing this book online.

CONTENTS

I - Beauty of Nature

Twilight

Each day there is such a time
which has for me an irresistible charm,
when the sun sends its last rays, then dies,
and misted shadows cast and spread far.

I like in such an afternoon time
to roam the streets, stop at water canals,
which mirrored surface sends sparks of light,
illuminating our faces and dim contours.

Shadows of twilight hide the every ugliness,
you don't see shabby houses or dirt behind the barrier,
yet every met entity seems to be more gorgeous,
because a bit smeared and as if more ethereal.

Windows of houses in daylight almost invisible,
in the twilight – become nearly fabulous,
reflecting rays of sunset as tinsel,
they are the endless spectators' glass eyes.

Immerse ourselves into the last golden rays,
traverse that street and park walking along arm in arm,
soothe outdoors our torn up nerves,
let peace surround us in that magical time.

Tempting Predator

Your fabulous appearance, colours
and shapes, attract many admirers flawlessly;
lured by the sweet promise of fullness,
stick to you passionately.

As if luminous crystals or droplets of dew,
to which they rush so viciously,
are the clever trap for their fate;
how transient is their happiness!

Greedily you pull your enticing feelers
winching them in your viscous embraces;
though they're struggling, you tighten your grip,
and decompose your prey into the prime factors.

Then full and ready to allure again,
you present your charms temptingly;
adorable from a distance and very fancy,
ready for anything – carnivorous sundew.

Walk in September

Greyish and gloomy is today's morning;
reluctantly I creep out of my cosy and warm bed,
rinse sticky eyelashes from the remnants of sleep,
to sit down to a modest, yet nutritious, breakfast.

Nothing worries me, nor particularly surprises;
I believe I have experienced everything in my life.
How to muster some enthusiasm and a little energy,
for frolics with grandchildren and for the rest of my time.

I choose the walk through the misty and deserted park nigh,
along winding pathways dotted with dried yellowish leaves,
which the September forced to the early falling,
yet, wind spread over the grass glossy from damp and paths.

From the dusky sky are sifting the midget droplets of the drizzle,
moistening my skin's thirsty and insatiable pores,
I have to watch out for worms and snails roaming on the alleys,
which left the waterlogged soil and its different holes.

But here the sun begins to wade through the foliage,
dropping onto the wet ground streaks of the radiant light,
and suddenly all around me is shining and scintillating;
the park comes alive and sparkles up with colours bright.

Even further, on the horizon of the sky, the rainbow displays,
and purifies all of its tints in the tiny drops of the mist,
both, eternal triumphal arch and symbol of victory,
light over darkness and life over death.

December Walk by the River

Let's go for a long walk by the River
along its southern stone embankment;
although the sky is scarily overcast and rainy,
take fresh air and some of the physical effort.

Gusty wind is dancing restlessly with water,
which hums noisily - raising and falling;
its matted and turbid, dirty-loamy mass,
slogs with a bang into the deserted quay pier.

Look, what a view! As from a marine painting!
On the platform – a flock of still cormorants;
one of them oddly spread out its wings
as a black bogeyman of a movie horror.

On the creased surface of the water gulls perched
dutifully submitting to the gambols of the rollers;
falling and hiding completely in pits,
or floating on the top of the lofty ridges.

Look to the right! These two rowan trees
are adorned with innumerable purple balls,
as a bride straight from the Lesser Poland
in her folk clothes with the strings of beads!

Do you hear the rumble that comes from the left?
It water pounds with impetus in the quay wall,
to suddenly be blown up like a fountain;
quick jump saves us from the cold bath.

On the right we are passing a row of silent houses,
adorned with colourful lights and reindeers,
that in anticipation of the magical holidays,
attract and enjoy our gaze with flickering lights.

In front of me, on the footpath, something shines;
hesitantly I bend and lift a trodden coin,
cleanse it from the dirt, puff at it three times,
and hide it into the tiny pocket for good luck!

River Thames

Oh, Thames, which cut London in half
and take your murky waters to the East,
you are the backbone of all its stuff,
you make this city the dynamic and alive beast.

I like walking alongside your winding bank,
watching your waters at different times of the day,
whether the low ebb makes you not a large mark,
or high tide - a fierce and powerful bay.

I often wander along the stone embankment,
admiring its characteristic warehouses and piers,
charming bronze statues and riverside gardens,
snowy swans and gulls in flight, or lurking on the water.

I also enjoy your meandering course,
which hides from a spectator what is ahead,
and that is why, and that is the cause,
to marvel your view and love you like a mad.

In the Moonlight

In the Mediterranean moonlit nights,
while the scorching and muggy air stands still,
when clothes stick to sweaty bodies,
we set out for long romantic strolls.

Steadily we followed a winding tarred highway,
illuminated by a pale light of the moon,
which as a kind of companion from the astral sky,
served us in our wander as a guide.

Dormant pens, yellowish lights of the settlement,
were left far away behind us in darkness,
as tracking a narrow path through meadows and fields,
we were climbing to the top of a distant mountain.

Perching on a flat boulder of degraded basalt,
we listened to the hum of grass and play of cicadas,
absorbing aroma of herbs and wild flowers,
admired the shimmering sea from afar.

Our eyes could reach the dark blue dome of the sky,
speckled with a swathe of twinkling stars,
and a human like face - the brass disc of the moon -
its mystical light extracted us from a dark background.

Oh, the moon - a witness of those dreams and fancies!
Why are you silent when I look at you at night?
Couldn't you anticipate the future events,
letting us believe that it would be like in Heaven?

Dense Mist

A milky veil enveloped streets and parks;
carefully we break through its thicket.
It sticks to our clothes, eyes and fronts;
unsteadily I grasp you by your hand.

On a white screen of tiny particles of water,
emerge dim lights of city lanterns;
people's blurred contours appear suddenly,
to dissolve in a silvery glow quickly.

Far away vague outlines of trees and houses,
clattering with a dull echo barking of dogs,
on the metal-matt water surface – shades of swans,
ducks and coots – as in an unreal dream of elves.

Ballerinas in tunics circulate on the pond:
the retinue of the queen Odetta embodied in a swan;
the black-white ducks – servants in her palace,
noisy coots – coachmen beside gilded carriages.

Suddenly everything disappears as the flock of seagulls,
bright and fast as lightning, falls from the skies,
emitting sharp sounds, damaging the tale's charm,
and penetrating the field of my vision.

At last the sun shines through the puffs of white;
scenery from the ballet *Swan Lake* disperses.
Its rays brighten and lift the curtain of mist;
confidently I step ahead – fear no longer!

Summer Downpour

It's pouring down today what drifts to my mind
the recollection: we both in the Planty in a summer rain;
a rare event in the record of my memory
when we went together without animosity.

People fled, hiding wherever they could,
only we were briskly pacing the band of roads,
displaying our smiling faces in the rain,
which viciously whipped and lashed them.

Soon, we were floundering in the ankle-deep swift stream,
gambolling barefoot on the asphalt pavement,
wielding in our hands the soaked sandals,
like water nymphs or picturesque ethereal naiads.

Dotted with hoppers and blisters the surface of water,
looked like a huge pot of boiling broth,
while we – dancing in a stream of the rain –
the two nut shells bouncing on the waves.

In the end, the sun shone brightly in the sky and earth,
drying and coating our figures with a film of vapour,
sending into space countless swarms of sparks
from paddles, wet leaves and metal railings.

Half a century later, in Edinburgh Park,
with my wet body beside someone else's side,
I recalled both of us, dripping with water,
in various circumstances but in a similar adventure.

Mini Black Panther

I hear rustling - a black shadow is embodying him,
barring the narrow footpath in the park.
Though I'm towering over him like a mountain,
he doesn't go out of my way nor turns its gaze.

His emerald eyes are staring at me boldly,
black hair glisten in the sun like a heated tar;
stuck stubbornly motionless, doesn't quit
this miniature black panther.

Where does it originate from - the saying
like this - which says that a cat is a fake pet,
as he can't withstand long human gaze;
gets away from a man turning quickly his head.

You're an example that it's a complete nonsense,
for it's me who first retreated from the contest;
though your fascinating eyes charmed me,
and tempted to remain there with you longer.

Vigorously I waved my hand in valediction,
spontaneously thinking of your successful hunts,
getting, however, with regret the impression
that you ignored my words the pretty boy.

Into my mind came dozens of your cousins,
which hunting for leftover stale nourishment,
were searching trash bins among the houses
of the far country, in which it lacks for people today .

There I was for them the last resort
for the fresh food served in the enamel bowl,
and for a peaceful sleep in the shade of my garden,
not disturbed by the cruel pranks of children.

Repeatedly they expressed their gratitudes to me,
submitting generous offerings of their successful hunts:
substantial lizards, rats and locusts,
left by them on the threshold of my house.

Perhaps this is no time to feel sorry for your plight,
when people - more cruel than any dangerous beast,
rape, injure and kill the defenceless and each other;
they are far from your true *felinekind.*

Tiny but Formidable Creatures

Such tiny creatures you can hardly see them, if at all,
yet, so powerful that can cause harm or even death;
whether poets should deal with them, write the odes
describing their extraordinary images or qualities?

They nest everywhere: at home, at work or outdoors,
threatening our raison d'etre almost any time, don't they?
Even while working on the computer can cause distress,
and bug you by its existence as nothing else in the world.

Even if you tried very hard: scraped, cleaned, washed,
wiped, you would not get rid of them or conquer; they
are masters of survival and reproduction - I shall not hide;
approve the fact that they are, even you don't like it.

Amongst the millions of different crawling, flying,
jumping and floating creatures, there is however one,
which although tiny but very popular, even admired
by a lot of people: kids, gardeners, artists, adolescents …

Discretely hidden in her crimson, black flecked cover,
looks like a funny daring knight in full armour from a tale;
although modest, but brave in the face of its enemies,
a defender of flowers and plants of our orchards and groves.

When with the wind this lovable beetle flies down on you,
tell her these few words: 'ladybug fly to the sky,
bring me a penny bun', then shaping your lips as a spool
blow her off gently as if it was some precious molecule.

Road through the Forest

Here begins the road leading to the shady forest:
in my youth I was going along it to school every day.
We are climbing steadily uphill together,
to get to our school's playing field from the rear.

The enormity of the trees and gloom ruling around,
associates with the secretive aura of the shrine;
here I feel as meagre and tiny as an ant or a gnome,
creeping among the foliage, fallen the last autumn.

The soft brownish bedding bends under our feet,
sunny spots enlighten darkness at the moments,
dropped down dry twigs crack under our boots,
the birds' chirping jingles in the unaccustomed ears.

The openwork arbour with a patina statue of Gutenberg
- the inventor of the metal fonts and modern printing;
we take a digital photograph with his figure along:
Mr. Johannes! It is also a kind of printing of our epoch.

Here's a glade with a beautiful view of the villas afar,
there's the gorge with a creaky, crumbling bridge,
on the slope of this hill I used to collect the forest lilies,
and down there appear the big wooden logs.

We sit on them displaying our faces to the sun;
in front of us sit a man and child on a beech trunk,
as if waiting for a performance or play to be shown,
in this charming amphitheatre immersed in the green.

22

Only a short walk along a lane leading out into the terrace,
at which were built some moderate stylish houses;
In the end we give a farewell to the dim and silent forest
- we are back again in the noisy and sunlit street …

II - Fun and Positive Emotions

Dancing with Cinderella

It was Grand Hotel in the royal town; the décor
in the old rich style, with elegant boxes on the sides,
which as a shapely coral atoll,
encircled the polished dance floor.

You came in the company for the night dancing;
food and a red wine gave you the colouring,
murmur of voices gently penetrated the sounds of music,
dim lights cast faint shadows on the floor surface.

Suddenly a handsome youth emerged out of the darkness,
and with a slight bow invited you to a merry dance,
touching gently your bare shoulder,
he led you into the middle of the spinning pairs.

Like the rapid flow of a river the time was flowing fast,
while you were drifting weightlessly in his arms,
forgetting all about the world and your comrades,
fancying a dream about princes and their ladies.

It was wonderful until that unfortunate moment,
when he confessed that it was your last parting valse,
before the dawn breaks, he had set up to his homeland,
and this celebration was the farewell with the place.

Dazed and pulled down from skies to the earth
he, swinging gently, led you back to the table,
then as Cinderella, hastily slipped out of the ball,
without losing his slipper on the way.

24

Inn

Guest! Cross my threshold and take a rest!
I'm waiting alone to meet you by the road,
ready to satisfy your hunger and thirst,
and give your anguished body repose.

Take a seat on a bench fragrant with pine resin,
or on a lofty stool next to the bar;
we've got the delicious snacks and lots of liquors
among which the leaders are beers of all sorts.

The band is superb, sounds like melodious bells;
plays lively polkas, mazurkas and oberkas;
it will make your legs eagerly lift you up to dance
by the side of the feisty playful lass.

The cheerful company and vitality of the music,
will make you, my guest, you forget all your sorrow;
leave behind the daily dullness of the present toils,
have fun and rejoice, because life is like a black hole!

It Must Have Been Her Guardian Angel

How could she avoid going to the party
celebrating the completion of half of her studies?
However tormented her persistent thought -
my boyfriend went away - will I go there alone?
There is a lack of guys in our year
in return for many of girls; ahead of me forlorn
sitting at a table and watching the dancing pairs.

A cozy room, a group of friends and acquaintances:
greetings, chat with a colleague from the senior year
with the impressive confidence and eloquence...
Thought in panic - soon the dances would start -
better for me to flee home as quickly as possible...
But at that moment emerged a stranger who snatched
her to the waltz, and did not leave until the party ended.

All around her was spinning; then could not remember
- was any of them saying something, or she slept?
She awakened in the cloak room when they dressed,
walked together along the street, then by the railway track,
until suburban electric trains began to ride ...

At the certain inevitable moment he walked away;
even though she did not hear anybody's voice,
she knew what he said: 'I think you can manage further?!'
She waved her hand in farewell - has never found out
who he was, and why he showed up on the *gala* of her year.
Now, thinking that it was her Guardian Angel, who came
just in time, to make that evening a special event only for her.

If Only I Could ...

If only my speech has sounded a bit better
- without this strange accent, foreign to you,
my talks were fluent and accurate as an arrow,
I would feel like a trout in a mountain brook.

If only I could choose right words correctly,
pronounce them perfectly as a native person,
I would feel beside you more courageously,
and wouldn't abate suddenly like a wound up toy.

If I wasn't afraid that I might be misunderstood,
I would try to tell you something of my interest,
to prove that I have great skills and some hobbies,
instead of having to be often ashamed of myself.

If only I could be able to charm you so much, that
you wouldn't take notice of tiny mistakes in my spiel,
I would pick out from my memory special words:
the expressions - light and vivid as spring poppies.

If only all of these above I could or be able to do,
my poems would be passable, sounded a bit familiar...
Although I would not be an outsider any more -
would I deserve to be called a more talented poet?...

A Friend of Mine

A friend of mine is tender and kind,
she doesn't quarrel in a rude way,
she shares with me her food and mind,
and knows exactly when and what to say.

A friend of mine never lets me down, but
she is beside me on the good and the bad,
she doesn't abandon me when a vile nut
denigrates and deprives me of my pride.

A friend of mine demands from me nothing;
we understand each other in mid-sentence,
I shall gladly share with her everything
without unnecessary words being said.

London Buses

Cut alongside in two, high boxes on wheels,
blocks of crimson on the graphite setting of asphalt,
inseparably captured our thoughts and visions,
promising comfort and a taste of adventure.

Let's sit down on the front seats of the top deck,
over the head of the chauffeur driving the vehicle;
these are the ones that I like the most,
here I feel as a chosen one looking for her lover.

Look at the cars, racing the same way as us,
but aiming to different places, known only to them,
admire the nice facades of the houses we are passing by,
the effect of imagination of many architects.

Look! We're approaching the River, glossy in the sun;
I know you like the grand bridges, stretched above it,
fastening with steel clamps the two opposite banks,
as if they wanted to lace up both parts of their city.

What a pity! My son, we have just arrived!
It is time for us to leave our vagrant comfortable nests;
for perching on them are waiting many others,
let's flutter down onto the roadside pavement.

Christmas in the Holy Land

Since Christmas comes near, let us rejoice,
despite all the shelling, despite all the bombs,
let us sing loudly in the one sound voice
the merry and bringing us hope song.

Ref. Jesus! We are still here in your Holy Land,
   waiting for your coming the Son of the Man!
   Show to this troubled part of the world,
   you are the love, beginning and end!

We, Christians of Syria, Jordan, Iraq and Egypt,
are the core and the true salt of the region!
We've lived here since human beings appeared,
we believe in Jesus, whose credo is love!
Ref. Jesus! We are still here …

Though evil powers and some bad peoples
hold all the cards in here nowadays,
we will endure, because you are our boss,
oh, our sweet Jesus, who also are God!
Ref. Jesus! We are still here …

Therefore, let us join our trusting hearts
in the one, impossible to tear, a strong cord,
that will defend us against the wrong, and
- our Saviour Jesus - will give us much hope!
Ref. Jesus! We are still here …

Sanctuary of Art

You are splendid in your form and in what you embrace;
I am fond of your roundness and beauty at first sight,
on several of my photos you make the lovely background,
to cross your threshold was the dream of my life.

Your classical, red bricked woven robe,
with the terracotta frieze of moulded figures,
mirroring the skies, panes of windows and the vast dome,
make me think of the abode of gods, the mighty Acropolis.

Exactly there, high, in your luxury interior edges,
I attached myself to the bulgy cupola roof like a bat,
admiring its design, the purple-velvet lodges,
the steep rows of seats and the ellipsoidal stage.

When the audience already filled the rows of each sector,
the rustling of leaflets and whispers died down,
lights quenched, except a huge beam touching the scene,
then musicians, as a flock of black-white penguins, came in.

From my loftiness - they all like tiny mechanical puppets;
whisked briskly across the strings of violins and contrabass,
blew in clarinets, flutes, oboes and golden trumpets,
following the baton in the effective conductor's hand.

Sunk in the soft chair, I closed my eyes with a sigh of relief,
my whole body absorbing the harmony of the sounds,
which with the ease of a warm summer breeze,
soothed piled up stress and expelled anxiety from my soul.

So, don't accuse me of desire to flatter anyone's taste
if I proclaim to all: 'I admire you The Royal Albert Hall!'
Let this magnificent monument of art last for ever,
and bring credit to its creators and profit for us all.

Face You Are Looking For

Among thousands of unknown faces,
you're looking for the one you dream about;
has only to you familiar features:
alluring lips, adorable eyes and a shapely nose.

To find this one is a great piece of luck;
not once you will be deceived, because
the face which seemingly resembles it,
after a time changes its countenance.

Although, as if selected, what bodes well for,
and though it still has lips like a flake of a rose,
for some reason, strangely enough,
instead of sweetness they exude poison.

The wonderful eyes which enchanted you,
by its intense colour and shape like almonds,
suddenly send you the hostile steel flashes,
and push away as prickly thistles.

So, baffled, you retreat your courtship,
and modify a bit your requirements;
admit willingly that not only the nice features,
but the inner beauty, too, in a face counts.

For, the harmony of body and soul, makes
the face, even if not so unusually pretty,
attracts others with its esoteric influence,
sending you the call – stay with me!

Low Expectations

If you wanted to speak to me,
I would have nothing against it.

If you gave me a sign where you tend to be,
I would go there without any doubt.

If you greeted me there warmly,
It would make me feel good.

If you drank with me a cup of coffee,
We would sit down on the bar stools.

If you talked to me about something,
I would listen and not interrupt.

If you preferred to hear my story,
I would have a lot to tell you.

If you recounted a bit about yourself,
You would become for me slightly closer.

If you without any fear clutched my hand,
It would be great and it'd add a charm to you.

Teen's Friendship

Regina! Why are you playing pranks on me at night?
You are coming and showing your childish face in my sleep;
for nearly half a century we don't know of each other's fate,
do you want to remind me of our school friendship?

Mutual learning and innocent girlish jokes and tricks,
the very first cigarette smoked together and a glass of wine,
the trips in the group of friends to the forest for berries,
talks about our future and outings to the cinema.

You have started earlier than I to adulthood,
your husband, though handsome, turned to be not the one,
who has given you the dream happiness and joy,
yet, two children pulled you down from an Olympus.

In those days split pathways of our common fates;
suddenly there was lack of the base to mutual acts and dreams,
each of us went the way of our own plans,
other people, and the stream of distinct events, took us apart.

So, what is the purpose of your rapid night visit?
Do you want to remind me of yourself or say something?
Why your face is so mortally serious and pale?
Regina! Is it so that you want to startle me?

It's Time to Celebrate

A star may be already seen in the darkened sky;
it's time to sit down at the table covered with the white.
Let us express wishes heartfelt and sincere,
share with each other the wafer and a kindly word.

It's time to start the Christmas Eve feast;
scarlet borsch with dumplings is waiting and smells;
fish, salads, kutia, cheesecake and gingerbread,
display their tempting shapes and delicious flavours.

It's time for us to encircle the slim spruce tree,
sparkling with colourful ornaments and lights;
let the flickering shadows as mysterious brownies,
dance on our faces seducing us with their magic.

It's time for joyful carols to soar high like birds
to the glory of the child Jesus and the Holy Family:
Mary - his mother and Saint Joseph; shepherds
and the Magi, who offered to Him their bows and gifts.

It's time peace replaced our doubts and daily concerns,
and well-being has arrived into our houses;
let us change our dwellings into a land of happiness
governed, as Jesus taught, by the commandment of love.

Revenge of the Gypsy

Tomorrow - a trip to Warsaw - our capital!
For you, it was to be a first time:
tickets bought, victuals in the bag;
we sat on a bench to rest for a while.

Not suspecting what was about to happen,
immersed in the sun heat and our fanciful visions,
we got startled by the plump dodgy woman,
whose motley figure arose in front of us unawares.

Clothed in a long floral skirt with flounces,
and a colorful scarf on her black hair,
with equally dark eyes in the brown face,
she made us turn towards her our alarmed eyes.

Fixing on you her penetrating gaze, she said:
'Gypsy shall foretell you, Gypsy shall tell the truth,
what awaits you in the future; enough a few zlotys
to learn my lass, what the fate holds in a fist.'

We sniggered at her words - then you replied merrily:
'I'm awfully sorry, but I have no money Gypsy!'
At the same moment the tip of your nose,
found itself in the steel grip of her fingers.

You screamed - she vanished like morning dew;
watching with horror the blackening of your nose
I gave a loud laugh, repeating once and again:
"Gina! Sorry! I know it hurts, but I cannot stop!

This adventure hasn't changed our travelling plans;
in the compartment train, your black nose became famous
and admired, because of the story with the vengeful gypsy;
talks about it and laughter accompanied us till morning.

Catlike

You remind me of a cat from your character
with this full face of yours and lovable mien,
and although without its glistening fur
you're so mellow, warm and pliable,
and even the same as it - unavailable.

For even though you like to be petted
and praised, you're rather difficult to master
- nobody else but you should be adored!
If someone doesn't like it - so what?
Let them think that you're self-centred!

For you're a being walking your own ways;
you won't allow to be tied to anyone's leg,
and only begged greatly you honour others!
Therefore I wonder how can you deceive me
so easily with your unsophisticated tricks.

It's probably because I really like cats:
their autonomy, wariness and slow closeness,
and even that cornered - they can scratch.
So, let the lady reappear at my place,
and doesn't treat me as a disgusting rat!

Easter 2016

Fleeting drizzle, gusty wind and suddenly the sun,
green bushes and thousands of daffodils by the road;
in such a way nature greets our Lord and Saviour
at the beginning of the capricious London Spring.

A few people on the bus - celebratory and festive:
clean-shaven men in the elegant suits and ties,
some women from Africa - how motley their goans are,
and fancy large turbans on the black fuzzy hair.

All of them hurriedly direct their steps to the temple
so as to celebrate the divine resurrection;
Jesus, who gave your life on the cross for them,
comfort them and ease their daily affliction!

Loud sounds of trumpets, a joyful choral singing,
and the words proclaiming the victory of life over death,
Easter - a time of the Christ's triumph and a new hope
for reconciliation, peace and love among all people.

Kulig

Four horses and a coachman in a sheepskin coat with a whip
in his hand, on the colourful sleigh in front of the train of sleds,
similar to an outstretched, restless, winding snake's tail,
are waiting like a flock of steeds on their full of vigour riders.

Swish of the lash raise the eager animals to a high speed;
hest gee! A sonorous voice of the carter carries far away.
The chain of sledges glides already along a beaten snow tract
- we feel the flow of cool wind on our rubicund faces.

A white madness has begun - juvenility has its rights -
merry screams, jumping off the sleds, sudden races,
wallowing in the snow, cheerful hooting, capsizes,
while the sleigh is scampering through snow-white spaces.

The dusk falls rapidly and only occasional roadside lanterns
cast faint-yellowish circles of light onto the snowdrifts,
however it is still white enough as to see extremely clearly
passed farms, roadside trees, black contours of inns.

Snowy fluff pours more densely, sticks to our cheeks -
we feel now as explorers, looking for the way to the pole;
luckily a roadside tavern invites us into its homey inside,
where the prize is waiting: food, cozy warmth and repose.

Nestled into the soft and warm layers of kindly bedclothes,
I dream a glamorous winter sleep of a polar bear
of a life companion which hugs to me in my snow lair,
small baby bears, and fat herrings that can be ensnared.

III - In a Family Circle

Mother of Yours

Loves you boundlessly as her own fate
without waiting for reciprocity,
devotes to you her nights and days
and doesn't count on your fidelity,
       Mother of yours.
Doesn't get cross or complain,
when you hurt her, swallows the bitter tears,
though her wounded heart pounds,
hides deeply her bitterness,
       Mother of yours.
Offers you an innocent and faithful love
without amorous passion and perplexities,
at any your beck and call she runs to help,
ready for the greatest sacrifices,
       Mother of yours.
Don't underestimate the affection of the one,
who you will never ever fail;
have an open and tender heart for her,
because there is no other like
       Mother of yours.

Family Home

Family home is a magical place,
that binds memories and the near ones;
when you desert it your heart tears,
the fear of insecurity simultaneously arises.

Those partings with home I've already had several,
always accompanied it undefined sorrow;
the life which I lead in them was like a moment,
that passes quickly and floats far away.

How many homes are waiting on my way yet;
whether they will be close to my heart?
I hope, in the future, I shall not disappoint,
and the life with the loved ones will make it right.

Ceremony of Your Baptism

We're standing at the church's gilded iconostasis:
your parents, the godparents and a few guests,
with you, our daughter, tiny and frail as a swallow,
the main actress – unaware of her role.

Here he is – both – the *pop* and master of ceremony,
approaching us like very, living God, bearded and robust,
ready to perform the eastern version of the rite,
which will make of our child the follower of Jesus Christ.

Some questions, replies, quoting verses and prayers,
circling round a brass bowl filled with holy water,
yet, I confused, with a lit candle in my trembling hand,
not understanding what is happening around.

Suddenly a spasm of sob wells up inside me
at the sight that tears my heart apart,
when the pop thrice immerses your little body in water;
the church's silence breaks at the shrill cry of my daughter.

In this way a new Christian has arisen;
only the notice of the baptismal name,
washing the symbolic dirt of inbred sin from your tiny clothes,
and our baby donning the snow-white dress and cap.

With a joyful relief I capture you in my arms
and dry your cheeks from the remnants of tears.
Let the Spirit of God shines brightly upon you always
and gives strength till the very last of your life's day.

Antique Timepiece

You! The stylish wall clock from my family home
which were timing of my childhood and puberty;
have you been spared by the hard time, the loyal slave
of his, or like us, you surrendered to the rules of eternity?

In our humble flat of the post-war Polish existence
you were a piece of almost inexplicable luxury
with your elaborately carved wooden case,
and the gold-plated hands for the fate measuring.

By days you presented your tempting chiselled charms
and were the admirable beautiful antique;
at nights you were becoming insistent, doing the ticking
sounds, not letting us enjoy our well-deserved rest.

Long ago, deserted, you disappeared from my life,
I know nothing about your further history record.
Do you still measure the period of life for someone
or live out your days, hidden somewhere on a garret?

Nobody can stop time, even you, if halt - exhausted,
but the present can be changed for eternity by our faith;
even the old timepieces can have souls,
so why human beings might not have them?

Farewell on a Railway Station

After a wonderful time spent at your home
I'm standing inside a compartment train.
You, with your teenage daughter beside,
waiting for my departure and to say good bye!

The wheels start to spin and the train moves a bit,
but soon it runs up faster gaining a high speed.
Standing at the half-opened window
I observe you chasing the fleeing engine.

Why is there much grief inside me?
It's neither my first nor the last farewell!
But this time my sorrow is intolerably high;
I cannot bear it and I have a good long cry.

People are sending curious glances at the sight;
ashamed I'm pressing myself into the corner seat,
covering the face under a light linen cloak of mine
I sob, then cry, bitterly cry like a child!

Why do I weep? I don't really know!
Is it a premonition of the inability for keeping the parole
to see each other the next year? Yes, today I may say:
I will meet you neither the next year nor ever!

After a month in another home and distant country
the doorbell is ringing persistently and loudly.
There is a postman handing me a mail notice;
I have to fetch a registered letter from the Post Office.

I take it with a trembling heart, then sitting in a cab,
tear impatiently the coarse and weird envelope.
And now I know my brother why I sobbed:
the prophecy is fulfilled! Both of you are dead!

Our Jubilee

Forty years for the good and the bad;
it is a big chunk of time, isn't it?
Is it possible, that I, that You, that We, my lad,
day by day are together, yet fit?

Difficult moments, wonderful days,
yet, we both are with each other, aren't we?
Tell me, whence this bond of ours takes,
which common life doesn't startle?

Maybe it is sex, maybe plain lust,
whether we are seeking profits?
Look into my eyes straight and fast,
and profess the truth, which heals!

Or don't say anything, just splice our hands,
endure in silence, which absorbs molecules
of our secret thoughts and desires;
let's come true our ineffable dreams!

Tiny Entity

Such long waiting, so many problems, and here
she is and looks at us with her beautiful eyes,

smiling as if to me, as if to her Guardian Angel,
with her gentle sweet smile like a delicate bluebell.

There is in this petit entity with her gorgeous tiny face,
in this small girl - our wonderful daughter,

all the richness of the world and the greatness
of the Heaven, pith of love and a need for our care.

When she pulls to me her fine little hands,
there is nothing more precious over my whole life.

I Would Not Be Able to Live Alone

The lonely walk by the River;
the crisp air, the water gleaming in the sun;
why, my heart, you pound so heavily?
Why, my eyes, you're becoming watery?

Though it is radiant and brightly outside,
today my soul is disconsolate;
gloomy thoughts are swarming in my head:
could I endure a lonely life?

No, I couldn't live on my own!
I think you know this for certain.
I wouldn't replace the man by a beast:
cat, parrot, dog or a Guinea pig.

I must have a human being beside me,
even if he was to be a blind or curmudgeon;
that I may not collapsed into silence,
that may circle around me, though a few words!

I couldn't be able to live without you,
even if our love would desert us at all.
Let's exchange it in its beautiful variant:
friendship – and let it stay with us till the end.

Our Asylum

Yes, it was this house and this lodging;
we arranged everything for the two of us,
entrusting it with our destiny
in anticipation of peaceful old age.

How we were nursing the feathering of our nest
with fervour and attention for comfort,
how we were constantly garnishing its interior,
and observed the flourishing of our garden.

That was our peaceful safe asylum;
the time therein – full of daily hardships and worries,
matters and thoughts circulating around us,
flowed tirelessly and unhurriedly as swans.

Hidden in the shade of our grapevine, in the scent
of the Damascene roses, lilac and jasmine,
the unaware time was lazily sipping through our fingers
in the company of the honey-eyed kittens.

Our ideal home! How do you endure parting?
Abandoned far away to an unforeseeable fate,
torn apart by the cruel war winds;
will you forever remain our *fata morgana*?

Our Enchanted Room

From a room in the loft of our house,
we have a view all around the city of London.
Lying in beds we may see the sun rays,
and slide our imagined bodies on their beams.

We may ride on different animal-like clouds
in the deep blue of the vast skies,
or watch through the telescope distant stars
that twinkle, sending us an inviting smile.

Through the windows facing the South-East,
we can see small villas floating on the water,
with royal swans, fancy ducks and black coots,
roaming in the sweet flags of the glowing ponds.

The opposite side of our nest-like room
takes our vision far away to the North-West,
where we can jump on the domes and roofs
of the *Gherkin, Cheesegrater, Pinnacle* or *Shard.*

Fortunately we can work, dream and play
in our lofty, colourful and comfortable shelter;
let's be happy, let's be thankful
for everyone who made it possible!

My Time

The best time – of which I am not aware;
I don't hear it in a ticking clock on a bureau,
in a hollow obtrusive silence,
in an urgent need for struggle,
in a pursuit of everyday life,
in the anticipation of your presence.

They are moments when it lets me be alone,
allowing me to forget about its existence;
I may chat with my friend on the phone,
go to an interesting place,
betake myself to a restaurant,
or do nothing at all.

Don't let the time govern our lives;
let it flow or rush wherever it wants.
It is worth spending some time
to snatch a bit of luck.
Now, give me a hug,
and a kiss for good night!

A Photograph from Childhood

An old photograph from my childhood - with the image
of a handsome mature woman and a little girl,
in a myriad of blossoms of an apple tree in the setting
that delightfully embrace them with the white and grey.

This image is emerging clearly before my closed eyes
when I sometimes reach back into the memory.
After all, it was a very, very long time ago,
when I was... five ... maybe six years old?

You, mom, in the dark tight dress, with a bunch of flowers
on your arm, standing close to me, holding by the hand
your child - a smiling blonde girl with curly hair,
and narrowed eyes against the glare of the sun.

Nothing disturbs the peace and beauty of the moment:
we both look like happy beings in the Eden,
though wearing the second-hand dresses - UNRWA gifts
for the poor people from the war-ravaged Poland.

It would suffice a small turn of the camera to the side,
to focus the lens on a pre-war shabby block - our house.
It's dwellers - German laborers in the Free City Gdansk,
worked out their welfare, gravitating towards the Reich.

A viewer of this picturesque image wouldn't think
that our families were afflicted by the lack of everything:
the necessary equipment, food, clothing and medicine,
also toys - I nearly didn't know about their existence.

The truth of this picture ... is merely half hearted,
showing in the reality only the more beautiful side.
So, what about the dreadful and less-liked part of it?
Although invisible, it's there, stuck in our heads!

Because the truth is just, cannot be manipulated;
you can't take a bit from one site of it, to another add.
It always, like oil, flows to the top at any rate -
even if someone forces it to silence or makes it fade!

Let us not instead of the hell and atrocities of war,
conjure up a romantic struggle for freedom,
yet, a repulsive image of devastation and lots of killed,
don't replace with a vision of the future better world!

Years of My Childhood

Sit comfortably in your chairs and close your eyes,
we shall transfer to the fifties of the last century,
behind the *iron curtain* in Central Europe,
when your grandmother was a little girlie.

Look at that grey shabby block on the corner of
two streets in the Baltic port city - Gdansk,
with a large rectangular courtyard - partly occupied
by gardens, partly - a playground for children.

Closer to the fence and entrance gate darken two thujas;
the shrubby plumose acacia cuddle to them its twigs,
which stems with droopy golden and dense flowers,
invite us to wallow in their scent our noses and lips.

Three gooseberry bushes are left after former residents;
like a flock of hungry defiant sparrows or blackbirds,
we often feed on them, not letting their berries mature
- filling our cheeks with handfuls of the sour fruits.

This little blonde who in the corner of the sandbox
pours golden sand, a brown hair, and two little boys,
create a harmonious pack on our common playground:
a place of cheerful fun, races, and innocent pranks.

You ask what we are playing - we have no end of joy,
as well as a time that nobody skimps on us happily;
in the lack of everything, including nursery for children,
we organize a variety of games and romps willy-nilly:

a tag, hide and seek, cells for rent, jumping from the roof
of the shed on a pile of sand, tossing and catching pebbles,

collecting mushrooms and wildflowers in the forest,
playing with a knife, climbing on the tree branches.

Only sometimes our joy replaces the cutting sadness
at the news of children dying in the dud explosions,
which like it usually happens with kids disappears soon,
as call on us the surrounding world and lots of adventures.

The yard and the nearby grove are a place of our frolics:
here every stick, pinecone or acorn can be replaced
by the magic fairy wand, a hedgehog, a puppet or a knight
from the superb land of unusual thrills and experiences.

When the moon and first stars rise to the darkening sky,
and bats fly in circles in the fading light of day,
voices of the mums calling their kids home can be heard:
Eve! Maciek! Janek! Danusia! ... (It's me) Time to sleep!

Marine Navigator

You loved vastness of seas and an infinite distance
navigating your schooner to the abundant fisheries;
you pursued the wind among the breaking waves,
admired gamboling dolphins in the water spaces.

Your nimble smack served you as the family house -
its meagre crew - for the easygoing matey soulmates;
your ship moored at the wharves of plenty distant ports,
but in every of them you were someone from outside.

Amongst the relatives - a rarely seen visitor -
the hearts of your loved ones often tore concern;
small gifts, postcards, short news - all were
a small compensation for the loss of peace of mind.

The sun rays and piercing winds bronzed your face,
tales of your marine voyages awakened our fiction,
though work at sea maybe is exhausting as nothing else
- it forges and hardens characters of young seamen.

You explored the trails leading to the fishing waters
to earn the daily bread loaf for your children...
Sadly the overland route turned out to be too narrow
- leading you prematurely straight to heaven.

Third Birth

For the third time I became a grandmother,
a miracle of the birth of a baby was fulfilled,
a new life was revealed to us in its nakedness,
a long awaited hope lay in its babyhood.

And so began the daily continual ritual
around the teeny, little, fragile babe,
because even though helpless - the all-powerful -
with his loud scream he forces everyone to obey.

You pulled me too, Adam, into this weary dance,
made me rock you and nestle in my arms -
oh my angel, a sweet memory of my motherhood,
those bygone hopes and the hunted down dreams.

Grow up and take on a dare my delightful child
as a funny koala from the eucalyptus grove,
be a continuation of our intricate fates -
our sequential joy and a favourite of the gods.

Our Conversations

How could I forget our unending conversations;
these different chats - friendly and confidential -
about everything and nothing, depending on the case
and its weight, carrying content - significant or small.

The warmest memories - those from the student's club -
whispered in each other's ear in which the words:
I love you, kiss me, and hug, sounded identical
to a warm breeze murmuring among the foliage.

Talks on walks, dancing parties, fantastic journeys,
or while drinking a cup of coffee in our old house,
once joyful and light, like seeds of dandelions,
at times gloomy and sinister as the sound of thunder.

Admit it! Our conversations somehow grew old;
with years slightly calmed down, became a bit empty,
lacking the former lightness, a tad of vigour,
spontaneity, confidence, even a little banality ...

I don't have in you a constant listener of my poems,
and you in me a partner to the boring political debates;
how good we both can't stand gossip or rude comments ...
So now - let me be alone with my own thoughts, please.

Unanswered Questions

Oh, sister! Tell me honestly, my dear,
how did you begin this journey of yours?
Was anybody waiting for you at the bedside
to show you the trail leading toward the sky?

Say! Whether, as your soul started to fly away,
she was feeling something or reacting anyway?
Is she only the glimmering bright glint,
or ethereal, opalescent, milky tinted imp?

My sprite! Answer me, whether you wandered
along a dark tunnel toward *the brightness*,
which as the embodiment of the divine love,
introduced you into eternity in the end?

I'd like to know how are you doing lately?
After being freed from the physical pain
are you happier from those whom you bereaved,
leaving them here in sorrow and loneliness?

Yes, I know my dear, these are such questions,
to which the clues are granted only to those,
who like you finally are going away into
the mysterious and irretrievable journey alone.

That House

Although I lived therein the quarter of a century
it rarely came to me in my thoughts and dreams,
yet I grew up there beside you, mum,
in the company of the dearest people for me.
Every day I ran into the steep staircase up to the first floor,
then standing on its narrow threshold
impatiently waited for the opening of the door of that house.

Already in the middle, bumping into the coal stove,
standing in front of the entrance, I examined carefully
with my nose the content of pots, pans and bowls.
Through the kitchen, serving also as a vestibule,
I rushed into the large square room, where an accidental
jumble of different pieces of furniture:
a table, iron beds, closet, a big trunk, dresser,
and a squat carved armchair, completed the decor.

This chair, standing by the big tile stove in the corner,
in which I dipped myself completely as a larva in a cocoon,
seeking in it warmth and a shield for my frozen body,
was my favorite piece of furniture and toy at the same time,
my teddy bear in the brown-grizzly dye.
Sitting there with the knees pulled up to my chin, I absorbed
all the vivid stories of my mum about the pre-war life,
seeing in front of me at a glance the large colourful rug
above one of the beds, antique clock by the narrow window,
closet, big mirror, dresser and the door of the second room,
on the background of the dull walls of indeterminate tone.

That prewar mirror hung there only until dropped
and shattered into thousands of tiny pieces
harbingering, in the words of my mum, that in our family
something sorrowful had happened.
Now I do not remember whether a mentally ill neighbour
fell down from the pitched roof on our small kitchen balcony,
or a message came from America, that my aunt had died -
the fact is that in this house I spent many more years,
in which apart from the painful moments were also joyful ones,
and the normal life of the family afflicted by the war went on.

Non Circular Anniversary

Today is our wedding anniversary!
From the early morning reminds me of it a bunch
of roses from my spouse in a vase by the window,
and my old mobile phone buzzing with the notification.
As for January, the day promises to be great:
bright sunny rays reach the round table
where usually we consume our breakfast.
Just now the question is asked: would you like
to go to lunch in the restaurant with us?
'Why not?' - I answer, and go downstairs
to our room at once.

Then - a quick shower, more precise than usual
makeup, new clothes received from Santa Claus
less than a month ago as a gift,
and I'm ready to move out of the house.
A short ride by subway and we are on site -
Canary Wharf - here was built a new station Crossrail
- similar to a great ship moored at the dock.
We walk through the lovely park located on its roof:
tree ferns of the Paleozoic period and the rest
of the greenery, make on us an amazing impression
- we take a few photographs here.

But soon after, we find that we are hungry,
so we head willingly to the Cafe Rouge
to a delicious French lunch.
After ushering us to the table a handsome waiter asks:
'where are you from?' 'From Poland' - we answer.
He boasts that he is Spanish, and his girlfriend
originates from Mazury in our land.

When I tell him which city I come from, he says
he has visited Gdansk, too, and at last he flatters us
saying: 'Poland is a beautiful country!'

While we are leaving he sends us a lovely smile
and waves his hand in goodbye; what a charming young
man - I think - wagging my gloves in response to him.
The young go shopping into the shopping center,
we, seniors, with our youngest grandson
dormant in his pram go further - by DLR to Greenwich,
then walking on foot alongside the Thames,
we toddle slowly home.

This is not the end of our fun as the tasty cheesecake
is waiting for us, and on top of it - a sweet alcoholic
cream named *Amarula,* which has messed up in our
oldish minds so hard, that oblivious to the fact
that the concert in the Royal Festival Hall, planned
as the main attraction of our celebration, awaits still us,
we politely go to bed to sleep earlier than usual.
Now is the next day! Damn! I feel sorry for that concert!

A Time Given

We both, and those moments, given to me heartily by you,
will remain in my memory for a long time,
since they gave me a lot - a jolly mood, nice conversation,
some reactions and your genuine enthusiasm.

As in a kaleidoscope changed streets, squares, buildings
- unknown to me so far districts of my hometown,
when from the inside of your rapidly speeding car
I was watching the views just passed by.

So will stay with me: a concert in the Oliwa Cathedral,
that beautiful park, where we wandered here and there,
either enjoying the wonderful exotic plants in the palm house,
or hiding from the sun to the openwork arbour.

And afterwards - climbing to the Gradowa Mountain -
raised tens of meters above the city, where our gaze,
slipping past the towers of old churches across roofs
of houses, was greeted in the distance by the blue sea.

At the end, a meal at the Thai restaurant in the Old Town,
where hastily satisfying my severe hunger,
I was looking into your cheerful face,
reminding me of that tiny girl half a century before.

Thank you, my dear, for the glamorous time given to me
generously by you; it will last within me as a souvenir
and a beautiful memory of both of us,
bathed in the sunlight of that radiant day.

Spring in Damascus

You asked me a difficult question: "Do you miss
Spring in Damascus?"
I did not answer you up till now,
for how did this question come to your mind?

The Spring is great when you bear it in your heart;
is independent of the season or occurrence.
Comes to you whenever it wants
with someone's friendly smile or gesture.

The Spring, which iridesces with colours of flowers,
is beautiful like a bride in a garland,
but what is left after those wreaths and ornaments
if we are not seeking therein feelings but idols?

I have the Spring here with me all the time,
because I have around me those I love,
whether I dwelled in Paris, Berlin, or Shanghai
I would feel equally happy having them nearby.

Because, what we all need, it is my dear,
a little compassion, goodness and *daily bread*.
If you don't have support or a safe place to exist,
do the luring visions or sentiments count for you?

Vacation in Two

A small town somewhere in the mid of Europe,
a train station probably from the times of Bismarck,
a tarred road leading from there through meadows
to a small secluded hotel on the shores of the lake.

This object entirely deserted in the late summer,
regarded by us as a gloomy castle, where we both
played the roles of a queen mother and little princess,
trapped by cruel cunning monsters.

We would sneak off from our apartment alone
to enjoy secretly the fresh air and sunshine,
then sitting on the bench of the wooden boat
we would row across the reeds and water lilies.

Laying on the bottom of the rocking vessel,
we watched white clouds flowing in the sky,
that like snowy rollers on the huge ocean,
drifted smoothly or swirled above our heads.

The cute princess found her suite on the lake:
a sizeable flock of swans that she fed every day,
but the old monster - the boss of the holiday resort,
after finding about it, forbade her to do that.

The reason - how trivial - these magnificent birds
were leaving huge piles of guano in the driveway:
whilst removing them caused a trouble for the staff -
hence the monsters willingly set us free in the end.

IV - Romantic Sphere: Dreams and Feelings

Besame Mucho

I heard a long forgotten song yesterday
and its first words: 'Besame mucho',
felt like forty years ago, when hand in hand,
we swayed to the rhythm of this melody eagerly.

'Besame, besame mucho', I'm humming quietly
and although don't know the content of the song,
just then I'm thinking about us – me and you – tenderly,
associating her wistful tune and our love.

I've imagined our young happy faces like living,
full of affection and sweetness of the moment,
as absorbing the soft sound of music, hungry of feeling,
we were snuggling together with passion.

Melancholy caught my soul in her tearful claws
moving my hardened memory hidden layers;
the nice recollections, if not brought by force,
may be the cure for complexity of the current events.

Dream Journey

Balloon flights – my unrealizable dream,
returning always when I spot their presence,
hanging on the foil of the sky – impressing
the coloured blown eggs dancing with a wind.

This journey, my dear, we must hold together
in order to share everything in half:
rays of the sun, swarms of the stars and a rain,
view of forests, lakes and wild fields.

We shall be up there fancying a dream of liberty,
racing with wind, lightning and birds;
we shall cross the invisible boundaries
without worrying about scanners and tickets.

Our love shall expand its wings broad
uninhibited by the human convention;
like Adam and Eve in Eden we will gain a fruit
of enjoying the independent selection.

We shall leave off our daily toil
lifting up ourselves to a rosy dawn,
we shall feel like the Creator, for a while,
suspended in the space-time of the blue.

Spiritual Wrestling

I don't have a key to your heart;
probably you keep it locked in a safe.
I cannot reach for your secret code,
or be able to become a skilful hacker.

Stubbornly my thoughts turn to the aim,
which I do not choose consciously.
How hard it is to bridle the fleet hope,
then soothe it and cease firmly.

Unruly it quibbles with reason;
like a screen reflects the logic of arguments.
The mind knows its own but it bends
under the pressure of the blind instincts.

What a choice should I make?
Both of them I will leave in peace.
Maybe the power of mind will ease with a time,
or the hope gradually will vanish.

Crystal Being

You are as the ornate crystal on the table in the corner:
shapely, delicate and brilliant – if there is such a need,
but a bit boring and forgotten after many years;
will someone enliven you with a touch of heaven?

In the lights of chandeliers, you send your fervent flashes;
any belly-shaped tulip excites your senses,
pity your touch is so cool and slippery -
is it that you contain too much water inside?

You were conceived in the burning heat of the furnace,
conjured up there of someone's secret wishes
and caresses; in your seemingly hard – glass crust,
resides easily crushable – a pure crystal heart.

A connoisseur of crystal will discover you without
any doubt; with delight take you carefully in his hands.
He'll transform the water inside into hot steam
with his sight, ignite once more – the flames raging in you.

Once Time Has Stopped

There was a summer when time stood still for us,
when we swapped days for nights,
yet, at night we set out for a catch;
when in the moonlight we were hunting dreams
floating on the silvery lake surface.

In those days we exchanged words to touch,
and the touch became our eyesight;
snuggling at each other we listened to the sounds
of murmuring reeds and grasses in the forest glade,
not caring even about eating – living on the wild
blueberries, mushrooms and bestowed on us fish.

That time – though passed, is not forgotten,
cannot be wiped or contradicted;
as long as our memory has not left us,
but remains alive – it may still last.

Is it Worth to Wait?

Another day of a nervous impatient waiting
for an unexpected turn of fortune;
one more blank card from the calendar,
landing in the rubbish can full of waste.

Hastily you are pacing rooms of your home,
to press the handle of the bedroom door;
maybe he's still asleep and you don't know it,
maybe everything might be changed yet?

But no! The bed is made and repellently empty;
you throw yourself on it weeping bitterly.
Streams of salty tears flow through your lips,
you wipe them with the comforting bathrobe.

Sorrow squeezes your throat like a steel ring;
you ask yourself: why he has left me?
Maybe I can repair all this awful misfortune,
but, where do I have to look for him?

At the sound of the bell you rush to the door at once;
who is it? A former friend, somewhat forgotten.
That's good! There will be someone to lament to;
why would you need one who didn't care for you?!

Gold Ring

It was just a tiny particle of precious metal,
scattered generously by the Creator of the star sky;
the small gold ring, placed on her slender finger -
after several years of acquaintance - by her admirer.

For her it had the value far greater than ores
from which it was elaborated with a big accuracy.
It was a symbol of their mutual great warmth:
amorous spells and imagined fabulous desires.

Its brilliance - like the light of the rising sun,
continually pleased her eyes and brightened the soul.
She could look at it with her eyes wide opened -
enjoying, yet, still awaiting for new emotions.

Their affection, as it happens in life, burnt out;
her darling grew unfeeling, then went to a new one,
and the ring from him became an unwanted load,
a subject of tormenting her wistful recollections.

In a fit of sudden grief, she threw it into the pond,
thoughts about the past changed to an active open life,
and because she had a real big heart of gold,
she found love, joy, and compassion another time.

With a Glass of Wine in Your Hand

You used to say: 'In this blue long dress,
with a glass of red wine in your hand,
you look exceptionally attractive,
like a Greek goddess, or a nymph!'

You used to say: 'On your smooth cheeks
dance golden-magenta shadows,
yet, in your eyes ignite fiery flashes;
I like those varieties of purple on your body!'

You used to say: 'Your lips like a butterfly,
drinking the sweet nectar from the flower,
are sipping the sparkling wine slowly and gently;
I would like to be in its place!'

You used to say: 'Your fingers hold the cup,
like slender columns the charming arbour,
we sometimes visit in the nearby park;
I envy the chalice of your delicate touch!'

You used to say... But, now, I miss such words;
Let's sit down in our favorite cafe at the bar,
so as to drink a goblet of crimson liquor;
I'd like to be compared to wine once more!

'Blood Is Thicker than Water!'

A banal narrative, one of many in this world,
because in it was he, she, and on top of it - the third,
the so-called marital triangle - unless you guessed it,
a dangerous configuration - no one can negate.

Although in the geometry - this figure is quite stable:
has a solid foundation and the appropriate arms,
but in social relationships - rather inadvisable,
because all in it is odd, and it's the essential concern.

For, when he and she, showed affection to each other,
the third felt rather uncomfortable and awkward,
and when they two were involved in a serious discussion,
she inevitably felt deeply offended and repelled.

So, the third, out of envy or the intentional perversity,
and she - challenging her husband because of a vanity -
began to approach each other more often and willingly,
showing mutual excess of friendship, even intimacy.

'Opportunity makes the thief' says the known saying:
here a friend of the one had stolen the feelings of his wife
becoming the cause of the tragedy in this story,
when he was caught in the love scene because of his drive.

Soon, along with his mistress, in bloody bedclothes,
they gave their last breath - next to a statue of Eros,
with which her husband smashed their heads in a wild frenzy,
crying in despair the words: 'blood is thicker than water!..'

Risk of Loving

You and that girl were so close to each other
after you chose her as a partner to dance one evening,
and made her think: I am important to him,
while meeting you at the parties and in your home.

Did you want to have her only as a devoted soul
for mutual chats, remote walks and friendly cuddles,
or maybe she was just a bundle of aromatic herbs,
serving you to relieve a pain of the former parting?

Your fairy tales that you were a surrounding vamp,
rather amused her greatly than caused any fright;
craftily you dragged her in your ambiguous game,
your boyish charm made her fall in love with you.

Your passionate kisses and hugs for goodbyes,
ignited in her zeal and the state of a tender readiness,
to giving you everything that a lover can present with,
without asking in return anything but mere reciprocity.

How cruelly sounded your unexpected avowal
that your sweetheart - the foregoing beloved girl,
suddenly appeared in your field of vision again,
so you must part with her... Nobody's to blame!

Were you scared of this genuinely great love,
and the inevitable risk coming with it; not being able
to sustain a deep relationship, you used her innocence
playing with her, and her first exceptional fondness.

Now seeing her somewhere, you hastily look away,
as if you don't want to know anything of her existence,
though with dignity and silently accepted your decision
putting to death of her barely born true affection.

Magic of Sight

What brings together two strangers:
similarity or diversity of their characters?
On this subject we hear different opinions;
I'll try to prove the one which is mine.

Decisive, it seems, is an urgent impulse,
which we reveal sending a curious glimpse.
It indicates to a strange but appealing person,
that it intrigues you or makes you charmed.

If you're shy, your eyes send swarms of arrows
of swift and furtive glances at their secret target,
and when you succeed to catch its sight's touch,
at once you become bolder and more tenacious.

Sometimes your eyes dragged in a silent awe
by the object of your craving attraction try,
as a spider fly, to ensnare it in the cobweb,
to attain a reward of the real approach.

The magic of your sight makes you're interested in
the one, who becomes nourishment for your fancy,
while it pushes you to further recognition
of the object of your later desires and fantasies.

Infatuation

A weekend outing to the country on the picturesque lake,
with dwarfish cottages hidden inside plenty of trees,
fell into a memory of a young pretty girl - because
there she met a handsome, middle-aged, p.e. instructor.

She applied her participation to get a swimming card,
not anticipating this as a particular twist of fate;
briskly arrived to the reservoir separated in the lake,
but when she saw him - fell - there was no turning back.

Cutting the surface of the lake, she imagined that
she's an ethereal nymph, and he a Prince Charming,
so, just only for him she danced in the cold water,
trying to attract his gaze and complete attention.

He, apparently unaware of what she was experiencing,
did not manifest any sign, or a slightest interest
in dripping with water, and flapping like a fish a miss;
handed her the swimming card, and casually congratulated.

Aura - how ferocious - that weekend did not showed off;
the pensive girl walked alongside the shore of the lake,
just there she accidentally encountered the instructor -
they exchanged faint smiles, and mumbled few words each.

At night, there was a dancing party in the resort -
she flew into the venue as on wings dressed up alluringly;
many fellows were willing to dance with a charming lass,
but the one she wanted - he danced with a more mature lady.

Thought: 'what an unexciting woman he chose!
"What a face she has! What an awkward silhouette!'
In the bed, realizing her defeat, fell into a heavy sleep;
after a morning walk, departure ended her adventure.

Yet, the image of him stayed with her and gave no peace.
In the end she got his address, and scribbled these words:
'I cannot stop thinking of you at all, Mr Chris...
I think I'm in love with you madly like a silly goose!'

Long after the relentless time blurred his image, and she
almost completely stopped dreaming about that man,
unexpectedly received a long-awaited letter, what more
- she found in it the very promising answer from him.

Yeah, remembered her, and he'd like to spend with her
wonderful moments - best, in the familiar to both place.
But, how could it be! All at once his charm has disappeared;
she sighed with relief, then put the envelope on the shelf.

Free at last, and radiant as the Spring, ran to her boyfriend,
threw her arms around his neck and hugged tightly to him.
But in her soul remained unfulfilled desire of compliance,
and the question nagging her from time to time: what if?

Your Fondness

Where has been your great fondness mislaid?
Have it been washed away by heavy rains, dispelled
by blizzards; has it burnt in the crucible of your hearts,
turning into particles of ash carried by the wind?

Have you become so self-assured
that oblivious to the necessity of care it needed,
you left it thirsty and undernourished,
withering slowly like a spring without influx of water?
Were your not sophisticated desires and wishes
written so carelessly by a stick on the water,
that they proved to be not possible to accomplish?

Though you want to believe that a thing depends on you
it is getting harder to look for the common happiness,
to make sure that something can be changed!
However, somewhere at the bottom, a dim flicker of hope
still glows in you, waiting for a stronger blow
which would kindle it again, giving you encouragement.

Hide and Seek

I remember sitting on a branch of the cherry tree;
pinkish flowers all around my body,
your black eyes as from an Arabian Tale,
seeking and asking - where has she gone?

You are calling and listening to every rustle,
full of hope for the ending of longing.
Where did I hide? In a floral paradise!
You will not find me without the magic lunette.

I am now one of the plenty of flowers
blooming on an offshoot of the cherry tree;
will you recognize me among thousands of weaves?
The power of your love will show you my place.

Summon all your senses for help:
your eyes as sharp as those of a falcon -
maybe they detect in the tangle your blossom,
when they view through this rosiness around.

Ask a zephyr to bring you the well-known scent
and show you the right direction infallibly,
or open your heart and listen to it attentively…
It beats in the same rhythm as mine, Benny!

Finally Silence Prevailed

It is the end - they stand facing each other
separated by a space of absolute silence
- thick and heavy like stone walls,
erected unknowingly by them.

But it was not to be like that, because
there in the street all began so nicely
when he asked about the art gallery,
and she responded to him politely.

'Well fortunately that's where I go;
if you want me to accompany you, I swear,
I can serve you as a fine tour guide
around the area and the venue itself.'

From that moment they rarely parted,
sharing sad and happy moments of their lives
- however ignoring the deepening cracks
that arose between them and still enlarged.

It is why they are now looking like two pillars,
avoiding each other's sight stubbornly,
and why they fell in this persistent silence,
with a touch of regret and bitterness sting…

ABOUT THE AUTHOR

Reader! If you already have this book in your hand, I presume that you are interested in poetry, and that you would like to know who has written this volume and why?

I am Polish by birth, and I graduated in physical geography from the University of Gdansk in Poland, although the most part of my life I spent in Syria, which through my marriage became my second homeland. There, in Damascus, together with my husband, we arranged our home and brought up our daughter.

In the meantime I was learning how to speak the language of the people among whom I lived. I, also, participated in the life of the Polish community there and honed the knowledge of English, especially when our daughter after her marriage, lived in London.

I visited this beautiful city in the winter 2003 for the first time, and already fell in love with it: its architecture, landmarks, the Thames with the grand bridges, and the people – open and friendly. When few years later our grandchildren were born, I was coming to London every year.
Periods of separation from the loved ones caused that I began to write rhymes on birthdays and holidays for my grandchildren, and later, also for other family members and friends. In such a way my poetry writing was born – beginning from rhymes and simple stanzas, to more various in their content and use of different words, satires and poems.
Since 2011, after the war in Syria had begun, I and my husband, came to live with our daughter and her family in London.

In the summer of 2013 I became a member of the Poetry Society in the UK, and Southwark Stanza (London), where I started to meet regularly with other poets and present my poems.

Since then, I wrote many poems: satires, lyrics, verses of narrative form, as well as of reflective nature, on varied themes and subjects. Two of them were published in the anthology entitled ***"Poets in the afternoon 2013-2014"***. Their titles are: ***"Twilight"*** and ***"Spiritual Wrestling"***, and they are also included in this book.

I also was chosen two times as one of six poets to represent Southwark against Brondesbury and Shrewsbury in the poetic events named **"Stanza Bonanza",** which took place in the Poetry Cafe in London in 2014 and 2015, where I read some of my poems.

A great source of inspiration to my poetry are: the beauty of nature in all its manifestations, interesting objects and people - their actions, behaviour and feelings. Some of my poems bring out the beauty in man, some other show his frailty and vices.

From the beginning of my writing I have already created a lot of poems that have gained an appreciation in the eyes of other people involved in the poetry writing. Therefore I believe it is time they were published and presented to a wider audience.

Our beloved ones, who gave us an asylum, cannot imagine our return to the country torn by the cruel war, so do we. Maybe, mentally I am becoming more British? And for sure I shall be, if you my readers, accept or even like my poems.

Author: Danuta Dagair

Printed in Great Britain
by Amazon

71612432R00051